gypsy

fortunes

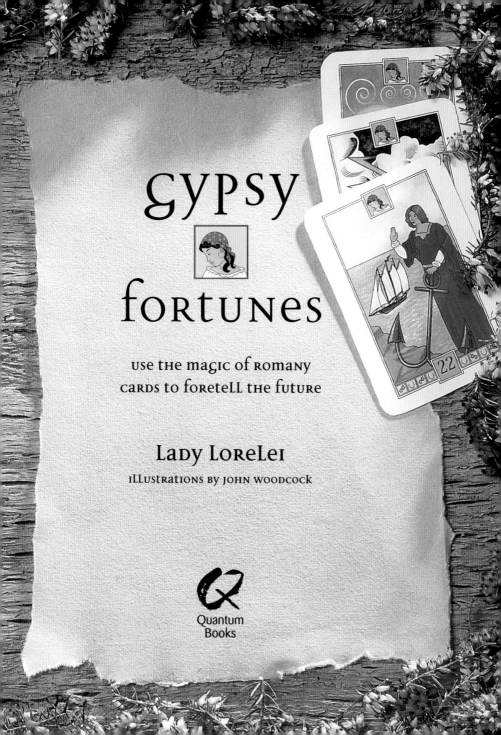

gypsy
fortunes

use the magic of romany
cards to foretell the future

Lady Lorelei

ILLUSTRATIONS BY JOHN WOODCOCK

Q

Quantum
Books

ISBN 13: 978-1-84573-521-0

This book is produced by
Quantum Publishing
6 Blundell Street
London
N7 9BH

Copyright © 2003 Quarto Publishing plc
This edition printed in 2013

QUAR.RFC

Project Editor: Kate Tuckett
Art Editor: Karla Jennings
Assistant Art Director: Penny Cobb
Designer: Caroline Grimshaw
Illustrator: John Woodcock
Photographer: Paul Forrester
Copy Editors: Penelope Allport, Claire Waite Brown
Proofreader: Mary Senechal
Indexer: Pamela Ellis

Art Director: Moira Clinch
Publisher: Piers Spence

Manufactured by Universal Graphics Pte Limited,
Singapore
Printed by Midas Printing International Limited,
China

contents

Introduction

Gypsy Fortunes is an introduction to tarot reading using 36 gypsy fortune-telling cards instead of the traditional 78-card tarot deck. The gypsy fortune-telling divination deck is technically a cartomancy deck, or one used solely to tell fortunes. The cards have simple and beautiful designs and each one is a powerful talisman of knowledge, and a key to wisdom.

The book introduces you to the old gypsy fortune-telling deck by outlining each card's symbolism and possible meaning and presenting a number of ways to read the cards. One-card readings are quick, easy, and eminently useful. Two or more cards can be used to answer specific questions, and you can even design your own readings. What is unique about this beginner's book

is the freedom from rules that it provides. Divination is an intuitive science, and the importance of the cards' symbols is determined by how the reader feels at the time of the reading. It also depends on the querist, a given situation, and the reader's instinct. Considering the cards' descriptions, meanings, and definitions is one way of reading with them; the card layouts is another way. Yet these are not the only ways. Like the gypsy in your soul, you will find your own way of reading with these cards, develop your own reading style and spreads, and find and trust your own inner gypsy.

Marie Anne Le Normand

The design of the old gypsy-fortune telling deck can be traced back to Marie Anne Le Normand, a cartomancer and deck creator. Le Normand is best known for her famous predictions in the life of Josephine Beauharnais. When Josephine was a young widow, Le Normand read her future in the cards, and declared that she would meet and marry a soldier who would later crown her Empress. That soldier was Napoleon Bonaparte. In 1807 Josephine convinced

Original Old Gypsy Fortune-Telling Cards, which were published by Whitman Publishers.

European card makers began attaching her name to their products.

In 1898, Camille Le Normand, Marie Anne Le Normand's great niece, published a book entitled *Wehman's Fortune Telling by Cards*, which she claimed was willed to her by her great aunt. In 1940, Whitman Publishers produced the Old Gypsy Fortune-Telling Cards, a deck of 36 cards, without suits or court cards but featuring images that were very similar to the additional art on Le Normand's deck. The new card art in this book further simplifies the imagery, to make the interpretation clear and allow for an intuitive reading.

Napoleon to have his palm read by Le Normand, who foretold their divorce and related details of his character and tastes. Napoleon asked Le Normand to put it all in writing, whereupon he delivered the document to the police, and, on December 11, 1809, had her arrested. Le Normand was detained for 12 days while Napoleon obtained his divorce.

Le normand and the old gypsy fortune-telling deck

We know that Le Normand wrote at least one book about her fortune-telling experiences. Skeptics declare this to be nothing but fantasy, stating her predictions were made up after the fact. However, in 1843, Le Normand died and, it was rumored, left behind a manuscript containing card designs and meanings, together with layout definitions. Soon after her death, many

Crystal gazing involves the use of a crystal ball to predict the future.

Gypsies (or Rom) have long been associated with divination and Tarot cards.

The art on the gypsy fortune-telling cards has a top and bottom, making the cards reversible, unlike modern playing cards, which, if dealt upside down, look exactly the same as when they are the right way up. According to the system laid out in Camille Le Normand's book, the reversals are absolutely necessary.

gypsy fortunes

Vast presumption exists in the public mind about the Gypsies. Many of us will conjure up a mental image of dirty beggars, palm readers, a decrepit but brightly colored caravan. The rich history and complex psychology of the Gypsy people are generally ignored, and discrimination against them is still practiced in many societies.

It is believed that the Gypsies (or Rom, as they call themselves), originated in northwest India, from where they moved to Persia. Despite ongoing persecution through the centuries, they moved from country to country until the start of the 1700s, by which time they had spread to every part of Europe. As a people, they represented the stranger; they were viewed as dangerous and often treated with great suspicion, introducing an element of darkness into the communities they visited. In order to survive, they often acted out the complex psychological projections that were placed upon them, becoming cheats, liars, and thieves, thus fulfilling the negative role attached to them.

There have been many large-scale, state-sponsored persecutions against the Gypsies through much of their history. Estimates are wide-ranging, but possibly up to 1.5 million Gypsies were killed in the concentration camps of the Nazi regime.

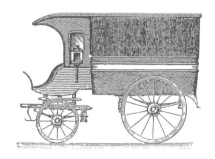

Misrepresentations of the gypsy people continue and contribute to negative stereotypes and characterizations.

There are many conflicting theories of the connection between the Gypsies and the tarot, the 78-card deck used for divination as well as gaming. More than one source declares that Gypsy fortune-telling was done by palm reading only. Likewise, more than one source credits the Gypsies with bringing out of India inscribed disks—a version of chaturanga, the precursor to chess. There are many books presenting the story of the origin of the 78 tarot cards, the 52 playing cards, and the wandering Gypsies. The earliest references to playing cards are documents prohibiting their use in Vienna and Florence in the late fourteenth century, which indicate they were popular in Europe.

The vast difference in the perception of the world by the Rom—a traveling people—should be appreciated. Oncoming weather, the length of daylight and moonlight, the ability to judge the character and honor of a stranger are all of vital importance. Certain truths reveal themselves again and again. The gypsy fortune-telling cards are a record of these universal keys to the truths, known by all who observe them.

Today's fascination with mysticism and the unexplained is reflected in the growing interest in tarot cards, crystal ball readings, and palmistry.

THE CARDS

In the 1940s, when the gypsy fortune-telling cards were first printed by Whitman Publishing, a consultation with a fortune teller would have been considered an act of rebellion, to be sought only by the desperate. Thankfully, at the present time, fortune telling has become a recognized profession and metaphysical science. By the close of the second millennium, fortune-telling cards had become useful self-help tools for introspection, self-discovery, and meditation. Now, the use of divination decks is evolving into a tool for critical thinking and decision making as we are bombarded by myriad valid choices, and possible options seem endless.

More and more people seek the advice and wisdom of the fortune-teller, the psychic, and the card reader. This book is an opportunity for you to learn the gentle art of divination as it has been practiced and taught by the Gypsies for thousands of years.

preparing for a reading

*O*nce you have studied the cards and have a feeling for how your conscious and subconscious mind relates to the symbols, you are ready to read with them. It is a good idea to start with one-card readings and then progress to two- and three-card readings. Then you can learn how to create your own spreads using as many cards as you need.

The easiest way to read the cards is on a clean, uncluttered, flat surface. I like a table covered with velvet because the soft, springy cloth makes it easy to handle the cards. You should create a peaceful card-reading space that is comfortable for you; a relaxed environment, with or without music, can help you to hear the voice of your intuition.

shuffling and cutting

Before each reading the cards are shuffled, during which time the querist and card reader concentrate on the specific question being asked. Cutting the deck can be a way of shuffling or the method you use to draw a card or cards. Camille Le Normand, in her book *Wehman's Fortune Telling by Cards* insists that it is done with the left hand because it is connected to the heart. Interestingly, Chinese acupuncture also shows a connection of the heart to the ring finger of the left hand. Modern card readers, however, tend to develop their own rules and preferences about shuffling and cutting, and when and where to use the dominant hand. Every card reader should concentrate on doing what feels right and best for him or her alone. I shuffle and cut the cards until I feel energy in my hands. You may choose to shuffle three times, or spread the cards out on the table and mix them around with your fingers before gathering them back.

When your shuffle is complete, you can draw the top card from the deck. Alternatively, you could fan the deck out

tHe one-card daily Reading

I cannot stress enough the importance of a good grounding in one-card readings. A single card is a window into the collective unconscious, and each card can answer any question in many ways, with layers of meanings and interpretations.

1. Concentrate on a specific question you want answered, then shuffle the tarot cards.
2. Cut the deck with your left hand, as this is the hand that is believed to be connected to the heart.
3. Turn the top card from the deck face up to find the answer to your question.

across the table and pull a card from the middle, or take a card from the bottom of the deck. Now, listen to your inner voice as you read the cards.

When you begin reading, bear in mind that the interpretation of all card reading is valid for a particular moment in time. When the cards are drawn, they reflect the energies and likelihoods of the past, present, and future. But the future is changeable, the past is subject to hindsight and rewriting, and the present is fleeting. People have free will and they change their minds. So any prediction is subject to change as time goes on.

practice Readings

After shuffling, draw just one card each day, asking the same question every time you draw. Do this for a fixed period of time, such as a week or a month, and keep a journal of the card you draw and what it means to you that day. You will be amazed at how many times you draw the same card. After some time, you will be able to see what the cards are telling you in relation to your question. Looking back, review your journal and take note of how much clearer and more specific the meaning of each card has become.

sample readings

Become an expert in the one-card reading, which is the building block for every other kind of reading, and you will easily assimilate larger and larger spreads, until you can read a full-deck spread flawlessly.

One-card reading

QUESTION: What do I need to focus on today?

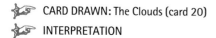 CARD DRAWN: The Clouds (card 20)

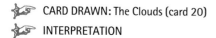 INTERPRETATION

★ My first thought is to check the weather. As I write, we have two hurricane systems headed across the Atlantic toward my state. The cloud system on the card is very tall and half-black, half-white, like hurricane winds, in contrast with the hurricane eye.

★ Another interpretation is that I need to change my focus from what is close at hand to what is lighter—more ethereal and esoteric. Perhaps I need to concentrate on spiritual matters like worship, prayer, or meditation.

★ Alternatively, every cloud has a silver lining. So if I feel that a cloud is hanging over my life, that I'm feeling some pressure or despair, I need to look for that silver lining, for the positive in the situation.

These are the three ideas that came instantly to me. Now look at the meaning detailed in the book.

★ "I am wishing and imagining."
Combine all these ideas to make a story or essay.

★ What I need to focus on today is my imagination. I should use the creative energy of the Clouds to plan projects or work on creative enterprises, or even to relax to a good show created by others. The Clouds card tells me to focus on the approaching hurricanes and what they could mean to me. It reminds me that I am not in control of the weather, and that it is time to remember who is. Further, I am not in control of the little irritations that will come my way this day, but I always have a choice: to see the dark side of the cloud, or to look for the brighter side.

REVIEWING a ONE-CARD READING:

Before bed, take a moment to review your day, and compare it to the notes you made when you did the reading. Was your first impression on target? Was it the third idea, the well-considered one, that turned out to be most accurate? Or, when you wove all your impressions together into a narrative, did that bear the closest resemblance to what happened?

Doing one-card daily readings in this way attunes you to your own intuition and teaches you what the cards mean to you. This book is a guide and a reference. As you work with the deck, you will find that you come up with your own more meaningful keywords and definitions for some of the cards.

OTHER RELEVANT QUESTIONS FOR THE DAILY READING:

How can I become a better card reader?

What does the universe want me to know today?

What do I need today?

What are my priorities for today?

What can I do to bring art and beauty to my life today?

ONE-CARD YES/NO READING

QUESTION: Should I stay in my current job?

🔑 CARD DRAWN: The Keys (card 4)

🔑 INTERPRETATION

★ The first determination made in a yes/no reading is whether you view the card as positive, negative, both, or neither. I consider the Keys to be a very positive card—the key to limitless possibilities. So, for me, the answer is yes. The Broken Mirror (card 33) would be no; the Clouds (card 20) would signify maybe.

★ You could flip half of the deck while shuffling, thus ensuring plenty of reversed cards. You then determine upright cards as signifying yes; and reversed cards as indicating no.

This card also tells me why this is the right decision.

★ I have taken years to get where I am. I have gained a lot of tools and benefits and now is the time to use them to their fullest. Leaving to go to another job would be turning away from all the knowledge, experience, and aptitude—all the keys—I have accumulated.

two-card yes/no reading

QUESTION: Will meeting X happen at time Y?

CARDS DRAWN: The Pig (card 8) and the Anchor (card 22)

Method 1

As with the one-card yes/no reading, you can determine the answer by the positive and negative values assigned to the cards drawn.

INTERPRETATION

★ I feel the Pig to be a very positive card, a yes, and the Anchor to have both positive and negative connotations, therefore a maybe. So my answer would be maybe yes.

★ Both cards give information as to why the meeting will probably take place at the assigned time. The Pig reminds me that we meet to share our realizations and discuss esoteric topics, even though the excuse is to share a meal. We contribute to each other's wholeness by positively affirming what the other has been doing. The Anchor tells me that, like carrying an anchor uphill, it will take effort to make sure we both know where the meeting is. We both have lots of things going on that might keep us from this meeting, but we plan to make a good faith effort.

Method 2

Assign specific definitions to the positions of the layout.

Position 1 signifies the answer (the Pig—card 8)
Position 2 signifies the reasons why (the Anchor—card 22)

INTERPRETATION

★ I see the Pig as a positive card, so the answer is yes. The Anchor indicates that for the most part, our activities are "docked" and anchored. We have a moment to lift up our heads for a breather and make this meeting happen. I am conscious that it will be a struggle to attend this meeting, either because of bad weather or because one of us may be carrying a heavy anchor like a deadline or other engagement. Most likely, it will be a successful meeting.

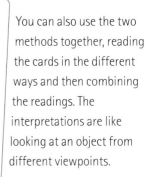

You can also use the two methods together, reading the cards in the different ways and then combining the readings. The interpretations are like looking at an object from different viewpoints.

thRee-caRd yes/no Reading

QUESTION: Am I on the right path?

 **CARDS DRAWN:**

The Safe (card 36)—prosperity

The Letter (card 13)—news

The House (card 3)—permanence

Method 1

Decide the positive or negative value that you feel about the cards and total them up.

INTERPRETATION

★ For me, the Safe and the House are strong symbols of prosperity, safety, and comfort, so they are both yes. The Letter is a maybe card. We do not know what is in the letter that she reads so intently. It could be good or bad news. So two yeses and one maybe indicate that it is likely I am on the right path.

★ Uncertain and stressful times often provoke the tendency to doubt oneself and seek a positive change for the better. The Letter tells me that it is all right to check new opportunities in the newspaper. However, the Safe indicates that I have money in the bank, and the House seems to say that I am in the right place at the right time. I am at home. There is no need to change and go elsewhere.

Method 2

Assign the positions the values of yes, no, and maybe.

The Safe (card 36)—Yes I am

The Letter (card 13)—No I'm not

The House (card 3)—Maybe I am

INTERPRETATION

★ The position of yes I am on the right path is a safe bet because of the Safe card. This card also indicates that if I stay on my current path, I will have economic security and prosperity.

★ The no position is uncertain and relies on news or communication from others. If a negative card like the Broken Mirror, or the Mice, appeared in the no position, the double negative of the position and card would mean a positive outcome to the original question. Had the Safe appeared in the no position, no would be the safe bet.

★ The maybe position is dependent on the House. With such a stable, strong card of comfort and permanence in the maybe position, I feel that my path is a strong and permanent one overall.

expanding the readings

You can use the principles discussed so far to make more specific readings. One good way to add clarity is to expand on the practice of assigning values to the positions of the cards, like you did for the two- and three-card yes/no readings. For example, you could decide to let the places signify past, present, and future or the body, mind, and spirit.

If you want to determine the essence of the reading, no matter how many other cards are in the layout, use the Camille Le Normand Surprise Spread (see below).

The Camille Le Normand Surprise Spread. Shuffle and lay out all the cards face down, leaving the interpretation of the surprise card until last, and see what it adds to your reading.

POPULAR THREE-CARD SPREADS

Personal
Body ★ Mind ★ Spirit
I need to . . . Think ★ Feel ★ Do
You ★ Relationship ★ Him

Choice
Option A ★ Option B ★ Magic Option
What you . . . Want ★ Need ★ Get
Good Choice ★ Better Choice ★ Best Choice

Time
Past ★ Present ★ Future
First ★ Second ★ Third—events or stages in order
One ★ Three ★ Six Months—adjust to any time frame you want

Situation
Situation ★ Obstacle ★ Outcome
Situation ★ Action ★ Outcome
Thesis ★ Antithesis ★ Synthesis

the challenge meditations

There are two main ways to use the challenges given in each card description. First, as you are getting to know and memorize the cards, ask yourself the challenge question and gaze at the card, noting down your thoughts in a journal. The challenge opens up a tangent to the meanings and symbols of the card. If the answer does not come easily and you struggle with it, you may want to work with that card for more than one day or meditation session. Answering the challenge question will help you understand yourself better, along with the symbols of the card.

The second way is to ask yourself a challenge question and let the old gypsy fortune-telling cards you draw tell you something about yourself in relation to that challenge.

one-card challenge meditation

Pick a challenge that you want to work on or that you are struggling with. Shuffle and cut the cards. Choose one card and interpret how that card answers the challenge question and how it relates to you.

QUESTION: What will I do with each moment this day? (The Sun—card 1)

⚜ CARD DRAWN: The Letter (card 13)
⚜ INTERPRETATION:

★ My first impression of the appearance of the Letter is that I will worry too much this day. As other people communicate with me, whether in person, by letter, by email, or by phone, I will wonder and worry about their hidden agendas and motivations. There is something about the woman's attitude in this card, the negligent way she has let the envelope fall to the floor, that fills me with unease.

★ Knowing this about myself, I can, instead, let things happen as they will and not be so worried. I will relax and enjoy the day as it comes, and value each moment as the opportunity that it is.

two-card challenge meditation

Shuffle and cut the cards. Choose two cards and lay them face down. Turn up the first card. Look up the challenge associated with the first card and meditate on it. What is your answer to it and why? Only when you have a clear understanding of the challenge do you turn up the second card and interpret how it adds to your answer to the challenge of the first card.

QUESTION: How can I deal with the challenge?

Card 1 signifies the challenge (the Train—card 34—where am I going?)
Card 2 signifies the answer (the Lightning—card 32)

INTERPRETATION:

★ My deliberate routines and goals, like the steady schedule of the Train, are taking me to a sudden flash or the surprise of a lightning strike. The expression "rude awakening" comes to mind. The only way to avoid the energy of the Lightning is to completely derail my plans and life, which is the equivalent of the sudden changes brought by the Lightning. So there is no real way to avoid it or prepare for it, except to nurture myself and trust that any change will be for the best. To have such a warning is a mixed blessing. It may turn out to be a sudden, very good change, after all.

summarizing the readings

As you do more and more readings of larger and larger layouts, you will want to get into the habit of writing a summary of your reading. You have already listed the definitions and symbols within the interpretation and related each card to the querist and the question. That is the detailed view. The summary provides a quick, concise statement of the main points of the reading. Go back to the original question and answer it directly. For example, for the one-card reading, what I need to focus on today is my imagination, to remain alert mentally, and always to perceive that I have a choice in how I view the day's events.

DeveLopinc the reADincs furtHer

Now that you have a taste of some common card-reading questions, layouts, and position meanings, you should take the time to become familiar and practiced with them. Then you can start building on them by adding new positions to the layout that cover additional aspects of the question. Soon you will be creating complex card layouts.

Decide exactly what you want to know about a given issue or situation before you ask your question. Write it all down and assign card positions to each aspect. Arrange the spread positions in order of importance and group them together in the ways they affect each other. For example, the main subject of the reading (usually you or the querist) often goes in the center, with all other cards of the layout touching or close. You might put cards about the past to the left, and cards of future likelihoods to the right. Use familiar shapes and easy patterns to organize your spreads. Start with a simple line of cards and move on to a grid with rows and columns; then go on to irregular shapes that are meaningful to you. Note them all down and soon you will have a library of useful spreads that you understand intimately.

Remember always to create a sense of the sacred by maintaining the utmost respect for the energies you work with in your card readings. Intend good for all concerned in every reading. Honor the cards, honor yourself, honor the question, and honor the answer.

When doing a reading, study each card, and absorb its symbolism and possible meaning until you have an intuitive feel for it.

This deck is a recreation of the Old Gypsy Fortune-Telling Cards printed by Whitman Publishers and inspired by the 36-card deck created by Marie Anne Le Normand. The original Whitman card descriptions are presented in the following pages as the Key Indication. The

THE CARDS

❀ ⚘ ☾ ❀ ⚘ ☾ ❀ ⚘ ☾ ❀ ⚘ ☾ ❀ ⚘ ☾ ❀ ⚘ ☾ ❀ ⚘ ☾ ❀ ⚘ ☾ ❀ ⚘ ☾ ❀ ⚘ ☾

symbolism of each card's picture is discussed in the context of today's modern world; then several interpretations of the card as it appears in a divinatory reading are explained. Should the card appear upside down or reversed, variations in meaning are discussed. Every card in this deck challenges us in some way, and these challenges comprise a resource of 36 possible questions to consider and meditate upon for personal growth.

The old gypsy fortune-telling deck is vitally important as a solution-generating tool, rather than merely a predictive tool. When you are struggling with a problem, a gypsy fortune-telling card can help you analyze new options and ideas and broaden your horizons.

1 The Sun — page 22

2 The Moon — page 24

3 The House — page 26

4 The Keys — page 28

5 The Sick Person — page 30

6 The Flowers — page 32

7 The Scythe — page 34

8 The Pig — page 36

9 The Fox — page 38

10 The Children — page 40

11 The Snake — page 42

12 The Rider — page 44

13 — The Letter — page 46

14 — The Queen — page 48

15 — The King — page 50

16 — The Lilies — page 52

17 — The Stork — page 54

18 — The Ring — page 56

19 — The Clasped Hands — page 58

20 — The Clouds — page 60

21 — The Dog — page 62

22 — The Anchor — page 64

23 — The Mice — page 66

24 — The Switch — page 68

25 — The Cloverleaf — page 70

26 — The Star — page 72

27 — The Cats — page 74

28 — The Sword — page 76

29 — The Flame — page 78

30 — The Heart — page 80

31 — The Cupid — page 82

32 — The Lightning — page 84

33 — The Broken Mirror — page 86

34 — The Train — page 88

35 — The Bride — page 90

36 — The Safe — page 92

1 ☞ The Sun

SYMBOLISM

A bright yellow Sun with many red rays shines above a river that flows from the mountains to the sea. The Sun has a pleasant, benevolent face surrounded by a white corona. The rolling hills are green and cool. The snaking river is warm and welcoming. The sea sparkles and blazes with reflected sunlight. The Sun is a most powerful and universal symbol for all cultures on Earth. Its rise in the east each and every day defines the rhythm of life. Therefore, symbolically it indicates a fresh start.

The Sun is the first card in the deck. Like the imagery of the Sun rising, the number one indicates a beginning or a new, fresh perspective. The winding path through rolling hills is symbolic of life's journey. There will be many ups and downs, twists and turns, challenges, thrills, and disappointments before you reach the perfect peace of the sea. The Sun also harbors a warning. The bright yellow reflection on the sea might be confused for a barren desert. The intense light of the Sun bounces off the water, burning from either direction the eyes of whomever is traveling the path, and making them look away from their goal. Then a turn in the path eases their eyes and they gain the strength to carry on, and once again face the truth in all its harsh, brilliant glory.

DIVINATION

Tarot Association: 19 The Sun

Keyword: Blessings

Meaning: Each moment of each day is precious. The Sun card is about the present and what you do with it. Appreciate it. Give thanks. Treat each new day with the joy and innocence of childhood, and take time to smell the roses. If you see life through the eyes of a child, it is infinite. A child lives for "now." Keep focused on your goal.

THE SUN'S CHALLENGE

What will I do with each moment of this day?

REVERSED MEANING

When the Sun appears reversed or retrograde, it indicates that a situation is too hot, and may burn out. Take care of getting too passionate, and thus becoming prideful, arrogant, and self-centered.

GYPSY WISDOM

The Sun shines on mud but does not get muddy.

KEY INDICATIONS

If this card lies at some distance from the subject's card, it predicts overwhelming worries. However, if the Sun (Card 1) is near, the troubles will be lighter.

2  The Moon

SYMBOLISM

*T*he light of a sickle Moon shines squarely over a river bridge. There is a small figure, perhaps two, on the bridge. It is almost as if the subject has turned his back on the sea in the Sun card and now looks toward the mountains. There is a single narrow tree on either side of the river, close to the bridge. What appeared green and full of life by the light of the Sun now appears ominous and threatening when seen through the dark light of one's own hidden mysteries. The Moon has a face, like the Sun, but instead of smiling down, this face looks to the side and contemplates the inner mysteries of one's soul. The blue mountains in the background look far away, perhaps signifying unattainability. There are some things we will never understand. The moonlight glinting off the river's surface has turned it bright yellow. This reflected light is soothing, but very hard to see by. The view all around is altered by the darkness. In this dim light we can't tell if the

shadow on the bridge is a lone figure worshipping the Moon, or two caught in the embrace of a secret midnight tryst.

DIVINATION

Tarot Association: 18 The Moon

Keyword: Illusion

Meaning: Overshadowed by the bright Sun, the Moon is perhaps the second most powerful symbol in human culture. The Sun lights the world, but it is the Moon that pulls the tides and the water in our bodies as well as the depths of imagination in our souls. The Moon card is about turning around to see what's behind you, what you've missed by the bright light of day, or what lurks in the shadows of your psyche. Is your information good and true? Be doubtful. Something important is being hidden from you.

THE MOON'S CHALLENGE

What can I see only by the light of the Moon?

REVERSED MEANING

Be still and allow the eclipse to pass. Things are not illusory. The shadow self stands in the brightness of the day. Some things normally hidden away have come out into the open, exposed to the scrutiny of others.

GYPSY WISDOM

The darkest hour is that before dawn.

KEY INDICATIONS

This card brings success in all enterprises. If it lies near the subject's card, an engagement or marriage is foretold.

3  The House

SYMBOLISM

*T*he House is white and three stories high, with red shingles and green shutters. There are flower boxes in all eleven windows. There is a circular window or vent in the apex of the gable, and three skylights or vents on the roof. This is a huge house where an extended family could live.

The House is symbolic of all things in life: the body, the family, possessions, responsibilities, health, and so on. The numerous windows represent the many places where light shines into our lives, and the various positions from which we can look out at the world. If some things appear dingy, dark, or dreary, pick another view. The House is where we retreat from the cares and harshness of the world. This is where we shed the outward persona we present to the world and become our true, comfortable selves.

DIVINATION

Tarot Association: 10 of Coins, Queen of Coins

Keywords: Security, home

Meaning: The House card indicates that you are secure. This is where, at the end of a busy day, you can let your hair down. It is where you were raised and where you raise your children. There is a permanence here that goes beyond the lifespan of the physical structure. Home is where traditions and life values are received and then passed on to the next generation. The House also reminds you to value the comforts and security of home and family life. The four steps leading to the door of the house suggest that a concern should be broken into four parts.

THE HOUSE'S CHALLENGE

What makes my house my home?

REVERSED MEANING

This is a warning that there could be something wrong with your house. Perhaps a feng shui consultation is in order. In any case, open all the windows and doors, or smudge them with incense, asperse them, and get the positive chi flowing again. Think about doing spring-cleaning, throwing out all the stuff that is no longer needed.

GYPSY WISDOM

The stronghold is taken from within.

KEY INDICATIONS

If this card lies near the subject's card, a wish will be
fulfilled. If it is at a distance from the subject's card,
the wish will not be granted.

4 ☞ The Keys

SYMBOLISM

*B*lack and white keys form a crossed pair; these are
positioned above two people, a watchman and a
maid, who each hold large key rings. Like a security guard
and domestic executive, these people have access to all the
doors and locks within an establishment or home. They are
in charge of the necessary ingredients for success. The key
or key ring is a symbol of great responsibility and trust. For
the cook, maid, or housekeeper, the keys open the doors to
the larder and the linens, metaphorically the doorways to
success in life. The watchman guards the treasury, the safe,
the items of great value, a metaphor for the things we
prize most dearly. Remember, these things needn't be
material, perhaps he holds the key to your heart.

The large keys above the people represent the bigger
issues in life. They are crossed, which indicates a turning
point, or crossroads. Perhaps it is time to make an
important choice or decision. Will we use the Black Key
to open door number one, or the White Key to open door
number two? We don't always know what secrets a key will
unlock, and we might later wish we hadn't used the key to
unlock a mystery. Yet how will we ever grow or progress, or
even accomplish great things, if we don't take a risk and
use the keys that life sends our way?

DIVINATION

Tarot Association: 1 The Magician

Keywords: Security, home

Meaning: The Key card indicates
that you already possess everything
needed to find a solution to the
problem. So look again at the
situation. Half of the solution is
defining the problem. You will find
that everything needed to manifest
your heart's desire is within reach.
Use the keys you possess to manifest
your desires in the physical plane.

THE KEYS' CHALLENGE

What door can I open with the keys
that I have?

REVERSED MEANING

You are not using the keys already in
your possession, or you are using
them for destructive reasons. You
may not be getting what you need
because you are using the wrong key.
Think carefully about what you think
you need and how you have been
trying to get it. This is a warning that
now is not the time to manifest your
desires in the physical plane.

GYPSY WISDOM

A golden key opens all doors.

KEY INDICATIONS

If this card is near the subject's card, there will be a great misfortune. If this card lies near the Dog (card 21), it indicates the loss of a friend.

5 ☞ The Sick Person

SYMBOLISM

A person in bed is attended by a nurse and a doctor. The Sick Person is a woman with long, curly, black hair. When a woman is used as a symbol, she represents one's inner mind, heart, and/or soul, whereas a man represents the external intellect and body that we show to others and most often show ourselves. Dark hair is stereotypically a sign of an intelligent woman; here, it signifies that this sick person has been healthy in the past and is intelligent enough to trust her doctor and nurse and follow their advice in taking medicine, rest, and exercise to get well again.

So often in Western culture we trundle along happily accumulating education, accolades, money, and material things. Then suddenly we realize that the externals mean nothing and we have starved our spiritual self. Although the emphasis of this card is on the Sick Person, the doctor and nurse are very attentive and helpful. Therefore, the card has a positive connotation of recovery, that whatever the problem, it will pass.

DIVINATION

Tarot Association: 5 of Coins, 5 of Cups

Keywords: Illness, disease

Meaning: The Sick Person card is a clarion call that yes, something is actually wrong, and it is time for you to right it. It's all right to accept help, indeed, it's probably a good idea, no matter what the problem. This card is a positive pointer toward recovery. You already possess what you need to be cured, so look forward to the time when you are well and whole again. Look for a solution inside yourself, but don't be afraid to let others help with the search.

THE SICK PERSON'S CHALLENGE
What will make me well?

REVERSED MEANING
You are not sick; however, by all rights you should be, with the way you've been carrying on. The reversed card gives you an advance warning. It's not too late to avoid ill health or some other difficulty. Take a look around your body, your life, your home, your job, to discover what needs proactive healing.

GYPSY WISDOM
A friend in need is a friend indeed.

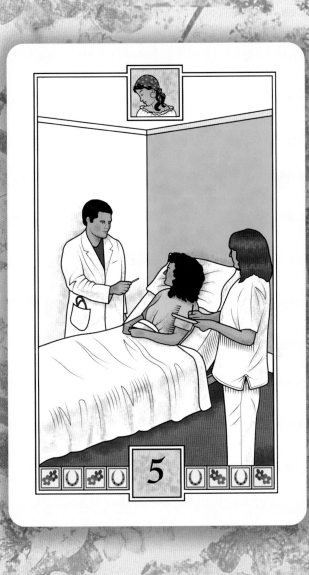

KEY INDICATIONS

This is a card of happiness. If it is near the subject's card,
it predicts the forming of a new friendship under
unexpected circumstances.

6 The Flowers

SYMBOLISM

*W*ildflowers of different colors and varieties are
displayed in a vase, towering over a wrapped
gift box. The flowers may have just been picked from a
field, or bought as a mixed arrangement from the florist.
They are in a pretty, green glass vase. Each flower is a kiss
of love from someone who cares about us. These are all the
things in life we can be grateful for but probably take for
granted, like health, clean air, water, food, and heat in
winter. The list is endless, and the bouquet is unlimited.

These beautiful, unique flowers also represent the
qualities and characteristics handed down to us by our
ancestors; the way we think and act; the abilities we have.
They symbolize gifts given to us by the universe, by the
Goddess, by friends, parents, and teachers. We are the vase
that holds all the flowers, all the gifts. We should be proud
of our gifts and give them to others.

The flowers are easy to see and appreciate, but what of
the wrapped box? It is a special gift that has yet to be
opened. Perhaps we are saving it for a time when we can
relish unwrapping it. This is the surprise gift that will be
there when we need it, the
hidden quality that we
never suspected we
possessed.

DIVINATION
Tarot Association: 4 of Wands

Keyword: Gift

Meaning: You are gifted and
fortunate. People love you and care
about you. You have many reasons to
celebrate and enjoy life. The Flowers
card is about acknowledging self-
worth. You are worthy of all your
wonderful gifts. Give your battered
ego a boost by naming your
wonderful qualities, as many as the
flowers. Look for hidden qualities,
shown in the unwrapped gift. There
is also a warning here. Don't forget
to water the flowers; nourish and
take care of yourself, so your
qualities can shine. Don't keep them
under wraps.

THE FLOWER'S CHALLENGE
What is that hidden quality that
remains wrapped up tight?

REVERSED MEANING
When the Flowers card appears
reversed, it tells you that you are
depressed and feel that you are not
worthy of recognition, praise, or joy;
that you have no good qualities. You
make a mockery of the gifts you
were given. Now it is time to
reevaluate how well you are using
the gifts and qualities you possess.

GYPSY WISDOM
One flower will not make a garland.

KEY INDICATIONS

This is a warning of great danger. The danger will be averted if lucky cards lie near.

7 The Scythe

SYMBOLISM

A boy in simple farmer's garb sharpens a scythe while standing next to a wheat field. Two huge scythes are crossed in a blue sky while puffy, white clouds float by. Traditionally the scythe is carried by the Grim Reaper, but here the scythe regains its practical importance as harvest is about to begin. The seasons are changing. It's time prepare for winter's long, cold, cruel months. The two scythes in the sky symbolize the duality of cutting away the unnecessary, bad thing and harvesting the good. A surgeon's knife can cut away a cancer, and by so doing heal a body. You must cull the rotten wheat to keep the good from spoiling. Sometimes we must sacrifice living things so that we may stay alive. A simple, harmful task can be for the greater good.

The boy is not daunted by the formidable task before him. Yet he lingers about the sharpening, pausing to consider the wheat field and its place in his life. Perhaps he is grateful to the Earth for freely giving such a bounteous harvest.

DIVINATION

Tarot Association: 2 of Swords, King of Swords

Keyword: Ethics

Meaning: Sometimes all choices presented to you seem bad, but you need to make the best choice you can, and not feel guilty about what that means. You must execute your decision. All you can do is your best. The worst thing you could do is not make a choice. It is time to remove the unnecessary things from your life. Thank these things for all they gave you, but put them aside. You no longer need them.

THE SCYTHE'S CHALLENGE

What is the way out of stalemate?

REVERSED MEANING

It appears that things are balanced by two choices or forces, but not for long. More choices will present themselves soon. Also, you have not harvested and gotten rid of things in season. Now they are dragging you down, rotting on the vine.

GYPSY WISDOM

A man must put grain into the ground before cutting the harvest.

KEY INDICATIONS

This card brings luck and success in all undertakings. If it lies near the Safe (card 36), it indicates good luck in business ventures.

8 ☞ The Pig

SYMBOLISM

A nude woman encircled by a green wreath dances on a cloud. She appears astonishingly like the World in popular tarot decks. Under the cloud, a fat, sad-looking pig looks at an empty food bowl. Mother Earth, the beautiful woman, is therefore symbolic of the eternal soul of every living being. When the temporary, material body dies and is buried, the soul or spirit lives on. So the body is like the pig, and the soul like the beautiful female figure. When we interact with other living beings, we must see the beautiful eternal soul on the inside, not the pig-like, temporary body on the outside.

Much of conventional wisdom pits the dour pig against the possibility of better things. The most unlikely and fantastic event will only happen when "pigs fly." Will we get a "silk purse out of a sow's ear?" But the symbolism is positive: behind the obvious, the ridiculed, sad pig, there is the chance of greatness, of better things to come.

The wreath or garland that encircles the female figure is indicative of the wisdom and experience of life that makes us an integrated whole. It represents the things that contribute to who and what we are.

DIVINATION

Tarot Association: 21 The World

Keyword: The eternal soul

Meaning: The appearance of the Pig advises you to look beyond the surface to the real value of the situation, and question on which side of the equation it falls. Look behind the façade. You are not seeing what's going on behind the front you've been given. You need to dig deeper and realize that you are not just the body you are in, and neither is everyone else. You need to focus on your soul's purpose, and integrate this with the wisdom of your experiences to become whole.

THE PIG'S CHALLENGE

What do I want to see when I look back on my life?

REVERSED MEANING

Don't dig deeper. Your situation is unsynchronized, discordant, and cannot be unified. Sometimes a pig really is a pig. Sometimes the façade is all there is.

GYPSY WISDOM

If all pulled in one direction, the world would keel over.

KEY INDICATIONS

This is a warning to beware of acquaintances. The closer the card lies to the subject's card, the more likely the scheming person is to succeed in their plan.

9  The Fox

SYMBOLISM

A thin, reddish-brown fox eyes the fine multicolored rooster on top of the fence. The fox's tongue hangs out with thirst or exhaustion. He has been circling the rooster for hours and is very tired. The fox and his antics are well known to the rooster. They have been through this barnyard dance before. Normally the fox can easily defeat the rooster and wreak havoc in the chicken coop. But the rooster has the advantage of higher ground, a symbol for higher purpose and righteousness. Although the rooster is small, weak, and ill-armed compared to the fox, he will win if he just holds his ground.

The Fox is symbolic of life's challenges, from major problems, like painful accidents and genuine misfortune, to petty arguments or simply a bad day at work. We are all faced with challenging situations at times, but we can choose how we deal with adversity. We can hide our head in the chicken coop and bewail evil fate that sent this fox to devour us, or we can stand straight and tall on the wall, and crow to show everyone how we greet this test with a carefree heart.

DIVINATION

Tarot Association: 7 of Wands

Keyword: Trouble

Meaning: This card is a warning of danger. Beware, watch out. Do not ignore the chance the Fox is giving you. Prepare yourself to meet any challenge, to fight from the higher ground. If you just persevere, you will survive and win.

THE FOX'S CHALLENGE

How will I outfox life today?

REVERSED MEANING

The battle you fight isn't worthy of you. You are not in the righteous position. You should be concentrating your time and energy on more important things. If you continue to fight this battle in this way, you are very likely to lose.

GYPSY WISDOM

He that seeks trouble never misses.

This card brings the promise of many and
lasting friendships.

10 ☞ The Children

SYMBOLISM

*T*wo children, wearing brightly colored play clothes,
plant flags in a sandcastle they have constructed. A
third child surveys their work from his seat on a tree
branch overhead. Whenever a child appears in a picture, it
is a symbol of many things, such as innocence,
imagination, growth, and learning. The children in this
card take us back to our own childhood, which we
naturally view with nostalgia, and hopefully with joy. The
flags sow the seeds of patriotism as well as separatism
in impressionable young minds, and are symbolic of all
things, helpful or hurtful, that children learn from
adults. This card takes us back to the attitudes that shaped
us and the reasons for so much of our adult behavior.

The tree is a symbol of life; it can live hundreds and
even thousands of years. The child in the tree is the
inquirer looking back at his own childhood. He is a remote
observer, watching and maybe even directing the work of
others. The three children have cooperated in a large and
complex endeavor, suggesting that life skills are acquired
on the playground.

More directly, this card may indicate our children, how
they are being raised, what they experience on the
playground, and what they are learning from the world
around them.

DIVINATION
Tarot Association: 6 of Cups

Keyword: Childhood

Meaning: This is about cliques, the
in groups, and belonging. Perhaps
you are surveying life from a
distance. Some are introverts and
some are extroverts, but you won't
find a common ground if you
continue to distance yourself from
the group. You need to look back to
your childhood to understand your
current behavior. The role you play as
an adult was modeled at a very early
age. Travel back in time to find out
why you are who you are.

THE CHILDREN'S CHALLENGE
Is it time to give up this pattern of
behavior?

REVERSED MEANING
You are not in touch with your
childhood (or your children). You are
not as innocent as you think you are,
or as you present yourself to the
world. The situation under
consideration has far more to do
with the present and the future than
with your past.

GYPSY WISDOM
Children tell you what they do, and
adults what they have seen or heard.

KEY INDICATIONS

This card foretells great misfortune through the
thoughtlessness of someone believed to be a friend.

11 ☞ The Snake

SYMBOLISM

From the temptation of Eve in the Garden of Eden, to the Sanskrit Shesh Naga (Ananta Shesh) that forms Lord Vishnu's bed, to Jörmungand, the Norse cosmic serpent, the Snake has been a powerful and provocative symbol in human culture.

Here, a very long snake coils down a tree. Its head and neck are free of the ground and thus able to strike. The snake tests the air with a forked tongue. The forest is very dark and ominous. The coils of the serpent graphically choke the life out of the tree, and this card is about the things that choke the enjoyment out of life. The forked tongue is indicative of lies, half-truths, and hearing only what we want to hear. The zigzag pattern on the snake's belly is the crooked path of selfishness and evil. The dark forest is where we find ourselves when we have turned from the path of right, goodness, truth, and light.

DIVINATION

Tarot Association: 15 The Devil

Keyword: Temptation

Meaning: You must examine your conscience and spirituality if you are considering a choice that you believe is too good to be true. The tempting energies of excess, addiction, and self-destructive behavior are present in the situation under question. Don't sell out for glitter, you are probably right, so beware of the hidden catch, and the strings attached. Don't let your weakness rule you.

THE SNAKE'S CHALLENGE

What am I doing that goes against my personal values?

REVERSED MEANING

You have come through temptation and can now realize what you learned from the experience. You have been saved from a wrong choice: perhaps you were strong and not taken in by the lies of temptation. The Snake is climbing up the tree toward the surface, rather than dragging you down to the underworld.

GYPSY WISDOM

Embrace the snake and it will bite.

KEY INDICATIONS

This card is very positive, as long as it is not
surrounded by bad-luck cards, such as the
Scythe (card 7).

12  The Rider

SYMBOLISM

*D*ressed for the hunt in a black hat, red coat with
tails, white jodhpurs, and black riding boots, a rider
jumps his white horse over a bush and a rail fence. It's a
bright day with high, fluffy, white clouds. There is a lake or
sea in the distance.

The hunt/jump takes years of training and an excellent
relationship between rider and horse. The rider is in control
and makes the decisions. He uses the reins to
communicate with the horse. A man alone could never
make the leaps and cover the distance, but partnered with
the horse, his strength, stamina, and skill are so much
greater. The strength of the rider comes from his
gentleness in training the horse. The rider convinces the
horse to carry him and perform such daring and graceful
athletic feats by training with praise and positive
reinforcement, not punishment. Too strong a hand with
the bit or crop ruins the horse and loses the contest. The
horse gives more and performs better for the rider it likes
and respects.

When jumping, the rider briefly leaves the ground and
appears to be airborne. However, the horse and rider are
still creatures of the land, not of the sea or sky pictured in
the background. The rider uses the strengths of his
element, and does not try to be something he isn't.

DIVINATION

Tarot Association: 8 Strength

Keyword: Control

Meaning: The Rider indicates
forward momentum in a situation,
moving ahead, overcoming an
obstacle. He shows that you have the
inner strength you need. Apply the
strength of love to this situation. Use
praise and positive reinforcement to
attain your goals. Be yourself.

THE RIDER'S CHALLENGE
To where do I ride?

REVERSED MEANING
The situation is out of control and
you need help. You lack strength
and coordination and are trying to
do something you do not have the
skill for.

GYPSY WISDOM
To fall down from a good horse is
even worthwhile.

KEY INDICATIONS

If this card appears near the Clouds (Card 20), news you receive will create many worries. If not, luck will come from afar.

13 The Letter

SYMBOLISM

A beautiful brunette woman, dressed in a gorgeous gown, is so engrossed in the letter she is reading that she has let the envelope fall to the ground. She stands beside a red velvet padded bench on a terrace overlooking formal gardens. She is completely unaware of her surroundings.

The implication is that the news in the letter is very important and informative, more so than her ordinary, everyday activities or the beauty and comfort of her surroundings. The news could be good or bad; what she desires to hear or the opposite.

DIVINATION

Tarot Association: 6 of Wands, 8 of Wands

Keyword: News

Meaning: This card indicates that news is going to arrive soon. You should pay attention and watch out for it. You are going to learn something unexpected, but the letter also warns you to remain aware of the unexpected. Things are about to start happening very swiftly, but don't become so engrossed in this situation that you lose sight of the other things in your life that are truly important.

THE LETTER'S CHALLENGE

Does this information really change things?

REVERSED MEANING

You have had or will have bad news, but that won't surprise you, you knew something was going to happen. Changes are happening more slowly than planned, or you have experienced defeat. The letter tells you to try a different angle. The information you need does exist, you just need to keep looking.

GYPSY WISDOM

Never try to write a letter while you are angry.

This card represents the woman whose fortune is being told. If the subject is a man, it represents the woman in whom he is most interested.

14  The Queen

SYMBOLISM

A mature, regal woman wears a golden crown and holds a scepter. She reigns over the land glimpsed in the background. A red heart frames her face. She also holds a fan.

This card symbolizes all things feminine, nurturing, passive, supportive, comforting, and healthy. She is the intercessor between the people and the land. She serves Mother Earth as well as her subjects. The Queen is the King's connection to the land and to his people. Her fan serves to cool his temper. She is the abundant harvest, the security of marriage and prosperity, the mourning of widowhood, the joy of sisterhood, and the perfect wife and mother.

The Queen may indicate the querist or someone in the querist's life, male or female, who has nurturing or mature emotional characteristics. She may be the kind friend or helpful teacher upon whom the querist can depend.

DIVINATION

Tarot Association: Empress or Queens

Keywords: Womanhood, abundance

Meaning: You are a good spouse and parent. You are in touch with and listening to your nurturing side, your yin energy. You allow yourself to feel the full range of emotions from grief and sorrow to great joy and love. A good friend will help you, or you can help others by being a good friend. Permit yourself to feel the security and comfort of a mother's arms, even if only figuratively. Hug your inner child.

THE QUEEN'S CHALLENGE
How do I prove that I am worthy?

REVERSED MEANING
You are either not in touch with or not trusting your feminine side. You see emotions as weakness and thus do not allow yourself to feel them. The situation is not one of abundance, though it could be if something is changed.

GYPSY WISDOM
A throne is only a bench covered with velvet.

KEY INDICATIONS

This card represents the man whose fortune is being told. If the subject is a woman, it represents the man in whom she is most interested.

15  The King

SYMBOLISM

*T*he King stands tall and proud in his ermine-trimmed robe, holding the scepter of office. His crown appears heavy with gold and jewels, a symbol of the weight of responsibility he bears, as well as the priceless value of the kingdom he rules. A large red heart frames his face, reminding us that the King is a person and has feelings, emotions, desires, and dreams.

In the distance, his castle sits on a high, lonely mountaintop, symbolic of the loneliness of his position and how he rules above all others. This is a card of fatherly energies and responsibilities. The King is the provider of the family. He defends his castle as its protector.

This card may symbolize a man in the querist's life, but also the more aggressive or assertive masculine qualities that anyone may exhibit: straightforward honesty, responsibility, conscientious ethics, ultimate mastery in one's profession or craft, or mature, well-grounded emotion.

DIVINATION

Tarot Association: Emperor or King

Keywords: Manhood, authority

Meaning: You are responsible and accountable. You are in touch with and listening to your stronger, assertive side, your yang energy. The energy of this card is about ultimate authority and responsibility for your actions, choices, and the effect thos actions and choices have on your subjects or dependents.

THE KING'S CHALLENGE

How do I exhibit authority over my own life?

REVERSED MEANING

You are not being responsible. You are letting someone else take responsibility for you and your actions and choices. There is a blockage in your honesty, ethics, mastery, or emotion. You have also not fulfilled your duties and responsibilites toward your dependents.

GYPSY WISDOM

With a king it is the same as with fire, stay neither too close, nor too far away.

KEY INDICATIONS

This card is an indication of a long life. If it lies above the subject's card, it shows the possession of high standards.

16 ☞ The Lilies

SYMBOLISM

*T*hree white lilies are potted and bloom next to a curtain at a window. Because they bloom in early spring, these flowers are linked to Easter and the many religious traditions that celebrate that time of year. Spring is a time of rebirth after the dead time of winter and speaks to us of the eternal life of the soul. White is a symbol of purity, of newness and innocence, of the mercy of having another chance to start over.

The Lilies card is symbolic of the relationship we have with our higher power. It is a reminder that our actions and choices will be judged at a later date, even if only by ourselves. For those who have a close, personal, interactive relationship with their higher power, the Lilies card is a sign of the immortal soul and its eternal relationship with that higher power. This life is a temporary time during which the soul is tempered by challenges, many of which seem like trials. The eternal afterlife symbolized in the Lilies is the reward for completing these trials.

DIVINATION

Tarot Association: 20 Judgment, 14 Temperance

Keywords: Security, home

Meaning: You are properly situated spiritually. You can depend on your higher power, and it is time to put your trust there and to meditate or pray. A difficult time will pass; it is a trial of life, and your knowledge of the afterlife is your reward for getting through it. The Lilies remind you to balance the spiritual and the material. You are in a good spiritual position now, but the importance of that must not be allowed to overpower your everyday life. The afterlife comes after life.

THE LILIES' CHALLENGE

How can I manifest the things I want in the afterlife in my present life?

REVERSED MEANING

You are not in good contact with your higher power. You have lost sight of the true purpose of your life. A situation is imbalanced and needs reevaluation.

GYPSY WISDOM

Life is not separate from death. It only looks that way.

This card predicts a change of residence and an advancement in business.

17 ☞ The Stork

SYMBOLISM

*T*he large, black-and-white stork stands on one red leg in a marsh. It's a lovely day with fluffy, white clouds dancing across the blue sky. The marsh is lush and verdant, with long-bladed grasses in the foreground and cattails across the water.

In spring, the storks return to their nesting grounds to start a family. The cry of a baby stork sounds much like a human baby, so it's no surprise that the stork is the symbol for a new baby. However, in this case, the new baby may not be the wailing kind. The Stork is the harbinger of good tidings, of family, and of the beginning of an endeavor, whether it be a new business prospect, a new relationship, or simply the will or idea to start anew. The stork holds its other foot close to its body, as if a little hesitant to put both feet in the water. It sneaks up on its prey, moving silently and stealthily in the marsh. This this is the card of undercover work.

DIVINATION

Tarot Association: Aces, Pages

Keyword: Do

Meaning: You are going to get what you want, so it is a good time to start trying and doing. This card is a favorable sign for pregnancy (though no medical pronouncement is implied), or the start of any endeavor, relationship, or idea. The Stork is a good sign for study, and for a shift in focus from the details to the full picture, or vice versa. Have faith in yourself, in others, and in your higher power.

THE STORK'S CHALLENGE

What needs to happen to bring this process I started to fruition?

REVERSED MEANING

The chance of pregnancy is low and now is not a good time to begin a new project. Because you are not in touch with your true desires or inner heart, you are not doing what is needed to accomplish anything.

GYPSY WISDOM

Storks like their feet wet.

KEY INDICATIONS

To the right of the subject's card, this card foretells a happy marriage. If it appears on the left side, it predicts an unfortunate marriage or a break in friendship.

18 ☞ The Ring

SYMBOLISM

A bride and groom stand with arms linked; she in a white wedding gown with a veil, and he in a black tuxedo and top hat. Their linked arms and the crossed golden wedding rings symbolize the union of marriage and that two are now one. The bride carries a bouquet of flowers, reminiscent of the Flowers (card 6). These are the gifts, strengths, wonderful qualities, and heritage that she brings to the marriage. Both the bride and groom have bare left hands. They have not yet taken up their rings. They are ready for the sacred ceremony of marriage, and to make their lifelong vows in front of their religious authority, their families, and their friends.

This card is about the public declaration of intent and identity. The clothes and all the symbols and trappings that we wear, like the Ring, represent a stamp of approval with a clear-cut definition and make us recognized members of society, culture, and humanity. The Ring serves to remind us that we are bound to society as well as to each other.

DIVINATION

Tarot Association: 5 The Hierophant (The Pope)

Keyword: Partnership

Meaning: You should rest assured that your hard work and commitment will make your partnership successful in the long run. Effort will be required, but the reward is security, support, and belonging. You have the approval and support of your community. The card also serves as a warning that society is watching. You are a member of a society and subject to its customs and laws.

THE RING'S CHALLENGE

You've got the official stamp—now what?

REVERSED MEANING

You neither seek nor have the approval of your community. Perhaps the situation you are in is not officially sanctioned by your religion, culture, tribe, or race. You must decide what is more important to you: the approval of your community or the voice of your heart.

GYPSY WISDOM

The older one marries, the longer the nights.

KEY INDICATIONS

Many pleasant friendships are indicated if this card appears near the Flame, the Heart, the Cupid, or the Bride (cards 29, 30, 31, or 35).

19 The Clasped Hands

SYMBOLISM

A noble man and woman stand in an open field under a bright blue sky. They are surrounded by trees and bushes, as if their business is open and honest, yet private. They are clasping hands as if they have agreed upon terms and are sealing the bargain. The man is dressed like a knight, swordsman, or cavalier, with a feather in his hat, black boots, and a sword poking from his long cloak. The lady has her hair gathered severely under a black hat. She is wearing a short jacket and a long skirt. Their attire suggests serious business, not fluffy romance. Both parties have removed their gloves to clasp hands. They are looking into each other's eyes, as if measuring the trustworthiness of the other's part of the bargain. Their clasped hands are magnified in the fluffy, white clouds above, emphasizing the significance of flesh touching flesh.

A handshake is a sign of trust and goodwill in many cultures. Even today, many business deals, agreements, and arrangements are sealed with nothing more than a handshake, because reasonable, civilized, honest people are indeed bound by their word.

DIVINATION

Tarot Association: 2 of Cups

Keyword: Promise

Meaning: I am bound by my word. This card is about striking a deal and clear communication. Two parties cooperate to reach a mutually beneficial goal, whether it is a business arrangement, partnership, friendship, or even marriage. These are the everyday practicalities of mutual support, the give and take that keeps the wheels rolling, all the promises we make in all our relationships. Learn to trust and depend on other people—and allow others to trust and depend on you.

THE CLASPED HANDS' CHALLENGE

Am I keeping my promise?

REVERSED MEANING

Don't make a promise you cannot keep. Now is not the best time to make a deal or arrangement. Further bargaining or a test drive is necessary, and you need to be sure of the warranty on this agreement.

GYPSY WISDOM

Bargain like a gypsy, but pay like a gentleman.

KEY INDICATIONS

If the light side of the Clouds card is toward the card being read, good luck is indicated. If the dark side is toward the card being read, hard times are in store.

20 ☞ The Clouds

SYMBOLISM

*H*uge, towering clouds move swiftly over a flat plain broken by a few trees and a clear, blue stream. On one side, bright sunlight illuminates fluffy, white clouds and the mountains in the distance. The other side of the Clouds is dark and threatening.

When we have a "head in the clouds" we are consumed with daydreams and wishing for things that are not within easy reach. The clouds represent those imaginings.

This card also encompasses the other cloud metaphors, from ill winds to the silver lining. The light and dark clouds can indicate a storm soon to come or one that has just passed. In any case, the situation is temporary and due for a change.

DIVINATION

Tarot Association: 7 of Cups

Keywords: Daydreams, wishes

Meaning: Developing your dreams can make them a reality and enrich your life. But the appearance of this card is a wake-up call, you can do too much dreaming, wishing, and hoping. The Clouds are a warning that the situation in question is on the level of a dream or wish. It's not reality and, like the storm clouds, it will soon pass, and change into something more clearly perceived.

THE CLOUDS' CHALLENGE

What are the ramifications of making this dream a reality?

REVERSED MEANING

This is not a dream. The situation is exactly as you perceive it, even though it may have a dreamlike quality. Your position is not going to change any time soon; it will stay as it is, and you cannot influence it.

GYPSY WISDOM

He who believes in dreams pastures the winds.

KEY INDICATIONS

This card denotes the presence of sincere friends. If it
appears on the dark side of the Clouds (card 20), it is
a warning to be careful when choosing friends.

21 ☞ The Dog

SYMBOLISM

*A*beautiful, sturdy dog keeps an alert watch over his master's property. We see the back of the house behind the dog who is guarding the back lot of the property. He takes his responsibilities very seriously, and is grateful and loyal to the family that feeds him.

Dogs have long been a symbol for loyalty, bravery, and even royalty, because of their cherished position as man's best friend and their many admirable qualities. Most dogs are good at raising an alarm, and many breeds do specific work or service for humans. But dogs are also very needy, and a great responsibility. We can learn much from the animals around us. The dog views every day as a new life experience. He does not hang on to grudges and always has a good attitude. We would do well to emulate the dog's content, in-the-moment worldview. The Dog card is associated with the Fool in traditional tarot decks, and like interaction with the court jester or fool of ancient times, interaction with a dog isn't serious; it allows a person to relax and subsequently forget his or her worries.

DIVINATION

Tarot Association: 0 The Fool

Keyword: Loyal

Meaning: You are faithful, loyal, obsequious, and a good friend. This card can indicate a good friend or someone who needs care. In traditional tarot decks, it is a dog who barks the warning to the Fool that he is about to step over a cliff. And in this case, the appearance of the Dog card is a warning to look before you leap. Realize that you are taking a chance that will have far-reaching consequences.

THE DOG'S CHALLENGE
Am I being loyal or obsequious?

REVERSED MEANING
The warning or alarm of the watchdog is still present, but mitigated by being reversed. So ignore the warning and carry on with your plans and activities, though they may be delayed.

GYPSY WISDOM
The dog that trots about will find a bone.

KEY INDICATIONS

This card predicts success in business enterprises.
If it lies near the Dog (card 21), it foretells the
appearance of someone who will be very trustworthy.

22 👉 The Anchor

SYMBOLISM

A woman with long, dark hair has one hand raised and the other on a huge, metal anchor. She stands high on a bare, rocky cliff. There is a large, masted sailing ship in the sea behind and below her. Her dress is the white of pure intent, the red of passionate discovery, and the green of wealthy prosperity. The woman has carried the huge weight of the anchor to a great height, and she holds up her hand in a sign of the success of the ship's voyage. The ship is in; the treasure is home.

An anchor steadies a ship when it is at rest; keeping it in place through the night and out of harm's way. It is also a heavy, dragging weight that drags at one, like the obstacles and challenges that slow us as we advance toward life's goals. This card is about bearing an immense burden, an immense treasure, usually out of love, like the burden of one's dependents.

In fortune-telling symbolism, a woman often represents the mind, heart, or soul of the seeker, the inner person or unconscious. The ship represents the body that carries the mind and heart throughout life. In this card, the inner person has scaled a high cliff, bearing a great weight, and yet is calm and fulfilled.

DIVINATION

Tarot Association: 3 of Wands, 10 of Wands

Keyword: Journey's end

Meaning: You are finishing a phase of exploration and it is time to land and become grounded. Make sure the burden you carry is a necessary one—borne out of love, not greed—and then be glad of it. Look toward the benefits, and the burden on you will be lighter. Understand that bearing this burden helps you to realize your true strengths.

THE ANCHOR'S CHALLENGE

How can I transform this dead weight into a burden of joy?

REVERSED MEANING

You have not yet finished exploring and need to investigate further possibilities. Now is not the time to anchor yourself firmly to one belief or plan. The weight of your burdens is too great; therefore, you must lighten your load and set aside some of that burden.

GYPSY WISDOM

He who will not be ruled by the rudder will be ruled by the rock.

KEY INDICATIONS

This card is a sign of loss or theft. If the card is near the subject's card, the loss will be recovered. Away from the subject's card, the loss will be permanent.

23 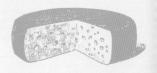 The Mice

SYMBOLISM

*I*n the dead of night a male figure with long legs runs away from a house into darkness. He carries a large sack of loot thrown over his shoulder. A ladder leans against the house. The man symbolizes the large, noticeable wealth that is in danger of being lost or stolen, like a car, a computer, or other tangible item. The ladder will be an obvious sign in the morning that something untoward has happened.

In the foreground, three mice eat stolen cheese under a culvert. The mice symbolize the smaller things that are also in danger of being lost, stolen, or forgotten, like monetary mistakes in the bank's favor, misplaced jewelry, or a supermarket coupon that has expired. The culvert is an existing part of the house and grounds. Yet it is also an unrecognized and therefore unguarded entrance, symbolic of workers, friends, or relatives who have free access to your material possessions and to your life.

DIVINATION
Tarot Association: 7 of Swords

Keyword: Theft

Meaning: This card is a warning on many levels. Either you are being robbed or you are contemplating robbing others. However, something you think was stolen may just be hidden. Loss is imminent. So the appearance of this card should be interpreted as a warning to be careful and remain honest. On a practical level, be sensible. Let friends and family know your travel plans. On a more subtle level, the theft or loss may be of freedom. Someone may wish to steal your peace of mind or sense of security.

THE MICE'S CHALLENGE
How does my lifestyle steal from someone less fortunate?

REVERSED MEANING
No theft has taken place and no intent to steal is imminent, though something may be lost or misplaced. Perhaps what is missing will be found. However, you are still warned to be on your guard.

GYPSY WISDOM
A thief believes that everybody else steals.

24 ☞ The Switch

SYMBOLISM

*T*wo children have very different reactions to the threat of punishment. The little boy scowls in anger and looks down in shame. The girl simply cries into her hands. Their toys, a wagon and a doll, are on the floor of the playroom. A handmade broom or switch waves in the air above them. We don't know what they are being punished for. Maybe they are both in the wrong, or perhaps they were playing nicely, her doll riding in his wagon, when a third child, or even an adult, knocked over the toys or started an argument.

Whatever the story, the appearance of this card is about confrontation and disagreement; miscommunication and unwillingness to cooperate. It is also about paying the piper and the cost of one's actions, whatever their original intent. What may have started as a harmless prank may end in serious injury or vandalism. Fire still burns whether or not we understand that it is hot, and sometimes the only way to learn is to get burned. Every action has an equal and opposite reaction.

DIVINATION

Tarot Association: 5 of Wands

Keywords: Strife, punishment

Meaning: The appearance of this card indicates confrontation, miscommunication, and an unwillingness to cooperate. It foretells troubles with regard to family matters, the workplace, or within a particular relationship. The situation in question could be one of those irresolvable cases where it is better to agree to disagree. The Switch warns you to consider the cost of your actions. What may have started as a harmless prank could end in serious injury. However, the Switch may simply indicate healthy competition or debate.

THE SWITCH'S CHALLENGE

I will forgive myself when I make mistakes.

REVERSED MEANING

You are not at fault, so your conscience can stay clear, although a disagreeable situation is apparent. The disagreement is not important and should resolve itself quickly.

GYPSY WISDOM

Do not throw the arrow that will return against you.

This card brings good news. If it appears on the dark side of the Clouds (card 20) and the Moon (card 2) is not near, the message will bring worries.

25 The Cloverleaf

SYMBOLISM

*I*n the foreground, three four-leaf clovers gently turn in the breeze. We see the patch they came from in an expanse of green grass. A small path leads back to a house nestled among the trees under a clear, blue sky.

The four-leaf clover, like the shamrock, is a symbol of good luck. But do we know what good luck is? Does the universe run on blind chance and destiny, or is there free will? Perhaps we can make our own luck. Instead of whining when things don't go our way, we should get out there and make it happen.

The cloverleaves on this card are blown hither and thither by the whim of the wind, indicating that good fortune can be taken away from us as quickly as it is found, so when good luck comes our way, we should hold on to it, not wait for the winds of chance to blow it away. The path leading from the house is very small and only traverses a small patch of clover. But we could make new paths over larger patches. We should search far and wide for fortunate opportunities.

DIVINATION

Tarot Association: 10 The Wheel of Fortune

Keyword: Luck

Meaning: Right now the universe is giving you a break. You are lucky and things are going your way. But you also need to make your own luck by getting out and trying. Circumstances are currently favorable for manifesting your desires. Still, effort is required to attain that dream house, dream car, perfect mate, and so on. But rest assured that you are on the right path and headed toward home, coming even closer to who you truly are.

THE CLOVERLEAF'S CHALLENGE
How do I define fortune?

REVERSED MEANING
Your luck will be better on another day and good fortune does not smile on the situation in question. There is an energy blockage in manifesting your desire, and larger external forces beyond your control are influencing the situation.

GYPSY WISDOM
Behind bad luck comes good luck.

KEY INDICATIONS

This is a good luck card. If it appears on the dark side of the Clouds (card 20), a long and unsuccessful journey will be taken.

26 ☞ The Star

SYMBOLISM

*E*ight stars make up this card—a large eight-pointed star is surrounded by smaller stars. Many of the world's religions and cultures use the star as a symbol of our connection to the divine and the infinite. Eight is a significant number in many belief systems, dating back thousands of years to the eight principal associates of Lord Krishna, as well as the simple mathematical truth of two cubed, and the physical orientation of the eight main compass points. The energy of the eight in this card reading is about fully embracing one's destiny, dharma, or purpose. You are no longer an apprentice but are approaching mastery in your endeavors, be they material or spiritual, physical or mental. But the Star is more significant than that. It builds on this "eight energy" and takes it to the highest degree, to the heavens, enjoining us to "reach for the stars," embrace our highest ideals, and make them reality.

The vastness of velvety, dark night skies dotted with starlight remains unreachable to mere humans, yet we see ourselves as tiny points of spiritual light in comparison to the infinite light of the godlike Sun and Moon. We are tiny suns—the same in quality, but tiny in quantity. Thus this card symbolizes the divine within our heart and mind, the source of all inspiration, knowledge, and wisdom.

DIVINATION

Tarot Association: 17 The Star, 2 The High Priestess, 9 The Hermit

Keyword: Inspiration

Meaning: You are receiving inspiration from a divine source and need to look inward for what you need, be it psychic vision, universal truth, or a fresh idea. Listen to your muse. This card advises you to slow down and be introspective. Take time to meditate and listen for the answer that is being given to you by a mystical source.

THE STAR'S CHALLENGE

Why do I deserve to be divinely inspired?

REVERSED MEANING

This is the only card in the deck that appears the same when it is upside down as when it is right-side up. So, divine inspiration, inner guidance, and depth of knowledge are fully present within you, though they may be covered or blocked at present. Give it a little time and trust, and your way will become clear.

GYPSY WISDOM

Stars are not seen by sunshine.

KEY INDICATIONS

IIf this card lies near the Dog or the Lilies (cards 21 or 16), someone will seek to obtain a favor through flattery.

27 ☞ The Cats

SYMBOLISM

A healthy, well-fed tabby keeps a watchful eye on her three playful kittens. The mother cat, or queen, wears a fancy collar that indicates she is cared for and cherished. One kitten scratches its claws on the furniture behind the mother. The other two kittens bat a ball of yarn on the floor before her.

This card symbolizes the sacrifices of motherhood: the mother cat attentively watches her kittens, ever ready to rescue them from their own curiousity when she might rather be out chasing mice on her own. Sometimes it's a great sacrifice to accomplish something as simple as finding the time to listen to a child. Cats are mischievous and playful when young. "Curiosity killed the cat" is an old saying. It is also said that cats have nine lives because of their amazing ability to survive the trouble they get themselves into. Sometimes it is appropriate to sacrifice ordinary duties simply to nurture and nourish the spiritual self.

DIVINATION

Tarot Association: 12 Hanged Man

Keyword: Nurture

Meaning: You do well to sacrifice your energy for a greater good because you nurture yourself as well as those around you. Think about sacrificing time, money, or energy now for future benefit. Remember the goal and don't give in to despair when the sacrifice becomes difficult. Cats are survivors and you too will survive this sacrifice you are called upon to make. Another interpretation of the Cats is to watch out for catty people and flattery, like the cat that rubs against you when it wants food.

THE CATS' CHALLENGE

What can I sacrifice for the good of myself?

REVERSED MEANING

Role reversal: now the kittens are taking care of the cat, the children taking care of the parents. The situation requires unexpected or unwilling sacrifice. The result of this sacrifice will not be of benefit.

GYPSY WISDOM

He who wills not to feed the cats, feeds the mice.

28  The Sword

SYMBOLISM

*T*wo crossed rapiers are echoed by crossed gauntlets hovering in the sky above. A dirt road winds its way through meadow and woods. Two men are hiding in the hedgerow; up to mischief, no doubt. They do not state their business in the open. Are they lying in wait to ambush a traveler on the road, to steal his money and goods? Their honor is certainly in question.

The two-edged sword symbolizes the good and bad sides of loss—the helpful cutting of the doctor's scalpel, and the hurtful cutting of the criminal's knife. The "sharp edge of the sword" describes one who has a keen intellect and sharp wit, or who makes cutting remarks. Thus swords are associated with intellectual and mental challenges and issues.

The gauntlet is protection while handling something as dangerous as a sword and is also used to issue a challenge, represented in the actions of "throwing down the gauntlet" or slapping another's face with a glove.

DIVINATION

Tarot Association: 5 of Swords, 11 Justice, Knights

Keyword: Challenge

Meaning: Be careful on your journey, but don't be afraid to take action when appropriate. You are under attack and must rise to the challenge. To do so, you must use your brain and trust your intelligence over your emotions. However, don't accept the duel if it is not worth it to you. Be conscious of the ways you protect yourself, that they are not perceived as a challenge by others.

THE SWORD'S CHALLENGE

What will you do if you lose?

REVERSED MEANING

Conflict and disagreement are present, but mitigated, lessened, or delayed. You need to be aware of this, but you can avoid it and move beyond it easily. You do not have to engage in the conflict yourself.

GYPSY WISDOM

Everyone loves justice in the affairs of another.

KEY INDICATIONS

This is a good luck card. It weakens the meaning of all evil cards near it and strengthens the meaning of all good cards.

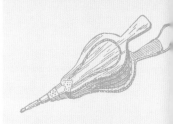

29 The Flame

SYMBOLISM

*H*ere we see a warm, red, roaring fire burning away in the hearth. To the side is a stack of wood, potential fire. The Flame heats and lights the room, and the smoke is whisked up the flue and out of the chimney.

Fire symbolizes courage, passion, strength, bravery, and energy. The Flame unites earth and air, indicating the union of passion and intellect. Like the Sword (card 28), the Flame is active, even aggressive, and therefore masculine. Also like the Sword, there is a positive and a negative side to the power of the Flame. Fire is a source of heat, light, and warmth. Its creation and use separate human from animal. On the flip side is its terrific, destructive force. Whether we consider natural forest fires started by lightning strikes, or fires started by accident or arson, the flames can destroy and leave nothing behind but black ash. This destructive force is indicative of the

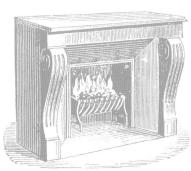

transformation that occurs in the cycles of the natural world, and in everyone's life. The Flame represents eternal change.

DIVINATION

Tarot Association: Suit of Wands, Clubs, Staffs, or Staves

Keyword: Energy

Meaning: You are passionate about this situation, or you need to become passionate about it. The Flame is a symbol of passion and energy and the willpower to get things done and achieve great goals. This card also indicates change. Perhaps the situation needs to be injected with energy or activity. Alternatively, if you cannot get passionate about it, then stop putting in the energy. You are headed for burnout.

THE FLAME'S CHALLENGE

Where is my comfortable distance from the heart of the flame?

REVERSED MEANING

Be very wary of whole-hearted passion. Instead, look to stable emotion to douse the flames should they get out of control.

GYPSY WISDOM

Sometimes you have to burn the quilt because of the fleas.

KEY INDICATIONS

This is a lucky card. An early and happy marriage and a happy home life are indicated.

30  The Heart

SYMBOLISM

*T*he Heart is deep red. It gives off a mystical, magical, wonderful, shimmering, multihued light. In ancient Indian and now New Age mysticism, the Heart Chakra is a wheel or ball of energy located in the center of the chest. It is the central chakra and governs emotions and relationships. It is also the center of consciousness and divine wisdom. Similarly, our religious beliefs tell us to listen to God in our hearts, whether we put our faith in our consciences, muses, the divine, or our own spiritual self.

The Heart is the symbol of our feelings and emotions and, by extension, our loving relationships. So when The Heart shows in a reading, we know that we are dealing with emotional issues, or that we must look below the surface for emotional motives and not worry so much about intellectual practicalities.

DIVINATION

Tarot Association: Suit of Cups or Hearts

Keyword: True heart

Meaning: You should listen to your heart very intently, and not so much to your head or intellect. This is your true heart, what you want, who you are, what you need, and who you love. It is time to extend love and caring into a relationship. Dare to love and nurture, and see that giving as your reward. Follow your heart. This is the path your heart would have you take. The Heart card may also point to feelings that were hurt in the past as the cause of present anger and sorrow.

THE HEART'S CHALLENGE
Who will I love today?

REVERSED MEANING
There is something blocking you from listening to your innermost desires and wisdom. This is not the path your heart would have you take. This could be a warning to protect your heart and guard it from harm.

GYPSY WISDOM
When the stomach is full, the heart is content.

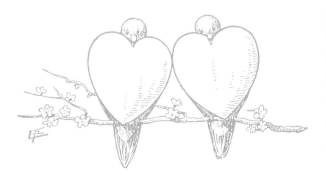

31 ☞ The Cupid

SYMBOLISM

A baby angel holds a bow and arrow ready to take aim. Celestial clouds in the background tell us that Cupid comes from heaven. He is not of this world, though his little feet touch the ground for a short time.

Cupid is the mischievous angel that tempts us by giving us what we think we want, not only in the form of a romantic partner but also in the form of money and possessions, praise, and achievements. This card is about telling the difference between infatuation and love, satisfaction and greed, appreciation and envy. Is the Cupid an angel sent to help you, or an imp sent to tempt you?

When this card shows up, like the Lovers in traditional tarot, realize that a choice must be made. Shot by Cupid's arrow, one is compelled to follow every romantic impulse. But there is always a choice between love and lust, between what feels good today and what's good for the long term. Every gain has a cost.

DIVINATION

Tarot Association: 6 The Lovers

Keyword: Lust

Meaning: The appearance of the Cupid advises you to consider your options carefully . You may believe you are in love, but could you simply be infatuated with this new relationship, opportunity, or item you wish to buy? Is it the best thing for your spirit and inner heart, or does it only satisfy the temporary whims of your fickle mind?

THE CUPID'S CHALLENGE

Wouldn't I rather eat nourishing, wholesome, brown rice than a chocolate truffle?

REVERSED MEANING

The chance to make a choice has been taken out of your hands. You have waited too long and the choice is being made for you. Not making a decision is its own decision, and therefore you are still responsible for the consequences of your choice.

GYPSY WISDOM

Love enters a man through his eyes, a woman through her ears.

KEY INDICATIONS

A surprise is not far away. If this card appears on the dark side of the Clouds (card 20), a disappointment will be experienced.

32 ☞ The Lightning

SYMBOLISM

A fearful lightning bolt slashes through light, upper-level clouds, and then dark, heavy clouds, to ground in the earth. You can almost hear roaring thunder following on the heels of such a close lightning strike, and feel the rain pelting down, drowning everything.

The Lightning symbolizes a sudden drastic upheaval in life, usually in our paradigm, world view, or outlook. It is often something drastic that accomplishes such a sudden change in one's thinking. Luckily, the trauma and excitement are usually quite survivable, and with hindsight, nothing more than a doorway to bigger, better, brighter things. When everything is going smoothly and well, our paradigm is not challenged and therefore does not shift. So while the upheaval is happening, try to remember that it's all for the best. Like a lightning storm, it will soon pass.

DIVINATION

Tarot Association: 16 The Tower

Keyword: Upheaval

Meaning: You are either experiencing upheaval, or a sudden, huge, and unexpected change is about to manifest. Change your paradigm. Look for positive opportunities in the midst of shock and surprise. Now is a good time to follow your instinctive self-preservation impulses, because your lifelong cultured habits are about to be challenged and maybe even broken.

THE LIGHTNING'S CHALLENGE

How can I prepare for the unforeseeable?

REVERSED MEANING

Upside down, the lightning goes from the dark clouds to the light. Therefore the upheaval is neither so sudden nor so severe. It's more of a large change or transformation than a traumatic life event—striking rather than electrifying.

GYPSY WISDOM

Weather is very seldom like the way it is described in the almanac.

33 ☞ The Broken Mirror

SYMBOLISM

A gorgeous, wood-framed mirror stands in a dressing room. Its glass is shattered beyond repair. In olden days, it was often the practice to keep a skull on a woman's vanity as a constant reminder of the temporary nature of life and physical beauty. A broken mirror is a sign of bad luck or even death.

In fortune telling or tarot reading we never speak of the physical death of a person, leaving that to the medical practitioners and funeral directors. Instead, the symbol of Death represents the necessary ending of a stage or process that must take place before we move on to the next stage and grow. It may indicate a time of grief, decay, and withering; but these things are necessary and vital to happiness, growth, and life.

Gazing at one's image in a broken mirror gives back a distorted, harsh, and inaccurate view. There's nothing else to do but to be rid of this mirror and get a new one.

DIVINATION

Tarot Association: 13 Death

Keyword: End

Meaning: The Broken Mirror foretells the end of a phase in your life, an end that is necessary to allow you to move on. Pack up and start looking for something new, or realize the loss and give yourself a grieving period, then a time of healing. The reins of power and responsibility now go to the next generation. Think about recycling the lessons you have learned, as opposed to throwing everything away, but get rid of what you need to.

THE BROKEN MIRROR'S CHALLENGE

What am I finished with?

REVERSED MEANING

The retrograde Broken Mirror suggests that a situation is not quite over. There is some small hope of mending things, but there is also a strong likelihood that it will end. Both sides of the situation must contribute tremendous energy to heal the rifts or cracks.

GYPSY WISDOM

Death pays all debts.

KEY INDICATIONS

This is a journey card. If the open door of the Safe on card 36 faces the Train card, the trip will not be successful financially.

34 ☜ The Train

SYMBOLISM

A long line of black train cars trails away into the distance, pulled by a large, black steam engine in the foreground. Steam billows into the sky from the smokestack and whooshes out from under the engine. The train runs along iron rails that are supported by wooden ties. The track curves, but the train progresses steadily on course.

The train is a manmade means of transport and symbolizes progress, from the Industrial Revolution of its birth to the information age of the future. We ride on the Train just as we ride the technological upheavals in our lives. The Train takes us forward, but during the journey we may let ourselves be transported without worrying about the final destination, or the stops along the way. The Train symbolizes the importance of choosing the right train and deciding on the destination; we must take control of our destiny. And remember, we also have the power to stop the Train, get off, and go home.

DIVINATION

Tarot Association: 7 The Chariot

Keyword: Control

Meaning: This positive card indicates that you are on track and in control of your life. It also portends a business journey, or a lot of travel in general. The Train is a positive card for business enterprises, so be assured that your career is going somewhere. Now is a good time for practical self-discipline, taking charge of yourself as well as others. Now is the time to move, and it is your choice whether that movement will be forward or back.

THE TRAIN'S CHALLENGE

Where am I going?

REVERSED MEANING

In retrograde, The Train is going uphill, so there is a great load on the engine. This suggests that you have a tendency to slip back a few paces for every step forward, but you have to keep moving. Don't let the clouds of steam blur your vision of your life, your purpose, or your business.

GYPSY WISDOM

Not all men are like trees; some must travel and cannot keep still.

This card foretells a happy marriage if the subject is unmarried. If the subject is married, there will be a marriage among friends.

35 The Bride

SYMBOLISM

A beautiful young woman reclines on a divan overlooking a lake. She is swathed in white from head to toe, and she holds a red rose. She also wears a red rose on her chest. She is smiling in happiness and love as she reads a letter from her husband-to-be. This card is similar to the Letter (card 13), but here the woman is very happy and comfortable with what she is reading. She has no doubt about its contents or who it is from. This is a letter that she will keep and cherish.

The Bride is a hopeful symbol for all things in family life and good relationships. She makes everyone around her happy with what they have and grateful for their many blessings.

The red rose is a symbol of passionate love that endures, although the rose itself fades. Like the letter she is reading, the bride will keep the red rose as a symbol of her groom's love.

DIVINATION

Tarot Association: 10 of Cups

Keyword: Hope

Meaning: You can be hopeful and happy. This is a great card for a wonderful marriage, or a passionate romance. An invitation is coming, maybe even a marriage proposal. Indulge in great expectations, because the future is favorable for this endeavor. Success and satisfaction in all your heart's desires are very likely. Anticipation adds spice to a relationship, so don't rush forward. Take time now to enjoy what you have.

THE BRIDE'S CHALLENGE

How can I achieve true success?

REVERSED MEANING

The hope of success is forlorn. Now is not the time to count on success, although it may still come, but at a later date. There is not a lot of hope for the given situation, and the pleasure of anticipation has turned sour. It is time to reevaluate your position.

GYPSY WISDOM

A good husband is healthy and absent.

KEY INDICATIONS

This is a money card. If the closed door of the Safe is toward the subject's card, money affairs will prosper. Otherwise, a loss of money is foretold.

36 ☞ The Safe

SYMBOLISM

A bag with the dollar sign inscribed on it is suspended over a green safe that has one door open. The bag shines brightly with the promise of gold and riches. There are other things in the safe—jewelry, stock certificates, deeds of ownership, gold and silver bullion, and more. The open door represents the art of putting more valuables into safekeeping.

Money and the valuables we lock away in a safe make us feel secure, prosperous, and protected. Other very valuable possessions include our physical health and well-being, which also contribute to feelings of safety and security.

We relate money to the elemental Earth, because in modern civilization it is what sustains, supports, and nourishes us. You cannot eat money, but you can use it to buy food or land on which to grow food.

Other valuable assets that we all have safely locked away in our minds and genes are the wisdom of our forefathers and the qualities of our ancestors. The Safe tells us to cherish and value all our possessions.

DIVINATION

Tarot Association: Suit of Coins, Circles, Pentacles, or Diamonds

Keyword: Prosperity

Meaning: The Safe indicates health, wealth, and permanence. You have everything you need to be happy and successful. Now is a good time to try a new business venture, make an investment, or buy something you've always wanted. Feel yourself part of history, and honor the wisdom of your ancestors. Take care of your possessions and they will take care of you.

THE SAFE'S CHALLENGE

How is prosperity an obstacle?

REVERSED MEANING

There may be an illness or disease. Something you thought would last and protect you forever is not permanent. You have misunderstood your forebears. Money is falling out of the Safe and going down the drain. Check for leaky faucets and unaccounted expenses. Perhaps now is a good time to tighten up your budget.

GYPSY WISDOM

When given a kingdom, the gypsy asks, what about bread?

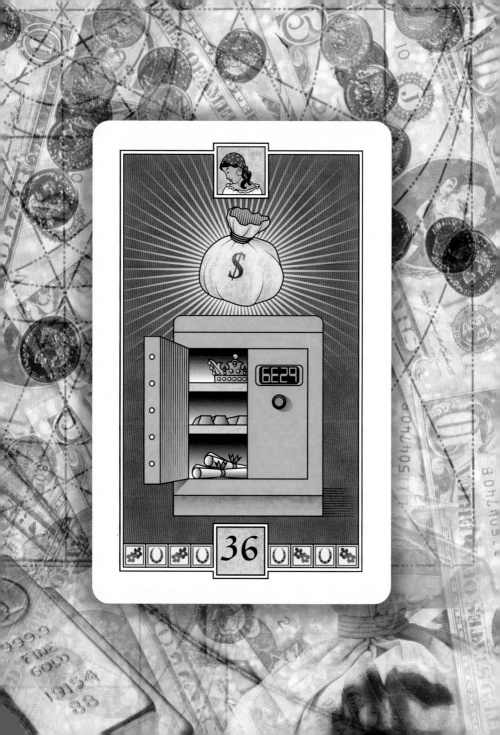

36

INDEX

✿ ❀ ☾ ✿ ❀ ☾ ✿ ❀

Resources

Buckland, Raymond, *The Buckland Romani Tarot*, Llewellyn, 2001.

Buckland, Raymond, *Secrets of Gypsy Fortune Telling*, Llewellyn, 2001.

Fraser, Angus, *The Gypsies*, Blackwell, 2001.

Le Normand, Madame, *The Unerring Fortune Teller: Containing the Celebrated Oracle of Human Destiny, or Book of Fate*, 1866.

Le Normand, Madame Camille, *Fortune Telling by Cards: or Cartomancy Made Easy*, Wehman, 1898. Available at www.eCDbooks.com

Le Normand, Madame Victorine *The Oracle of Human Destiny or the Unerring Fortune Teller*, 1825.

Le Normand, Mlle M. A. (Marie Anne), *Les Souvenirs Prophétiques d'une Sibylle, sur les Causes Secrètes de son Arrestation, Le II Décembre 1809*, 1814.

Le Normand, Mlle M. A. (Marie Anne), *Memoirs Historiques et Secrets de l'Impératrice Josephine*, 1827.

Gypsy wisdom websites
www.tarotgoddess.net
www.romani.org
www.gypsyloresociety.org
www.gypsyblues.com

Credits

Quarto would like to thank the following for supplying pictures reproduced in this book:

Charles Walker/TopFoto 7br, 8tl, 9br

(Key: b = bottom, t = top, r = right, l = left)

All other photographs and illustrations are the copyright of Quarto. While every effort has been made to credit contributors, we would like to apologize in advance if there have been any omissions or errors.